Bodies in Spaces

ETH Zurich, Chair of Gion A. Caminada (ed.)

Franziska Wittmann

Bodies in Spaces

Quart Publishers

Bodies in Spaces

Author: Franziska Wittmann
Editor:
Chair of Gion A. Caminada (ed.),
ETH Zurich
Graphic design: Franziska Wittmann
Graphical layout: Franziska Wittmann /
Quart Publishers, Linus Wirz
English translation: Benjamin Liebelt, Berlin
Lithos: Printeria, Lucerne
Printing: Printer Trento S.R.L., Trento

© Copyright 2019
Franziska Wittmann,
Gion A. Caminada and
Quart Verlag Luzern
All rights reserved
ISBN 978-3-03761-212-5

This book is also published in German / Ebenfalls
publiziert in Deutsch (ISBN 978-3-03761-210-1)

Quart Verlag GmbH
Denkmalstrasse 2, CH-6006 Luzern
books@quart.ch, www.quart.ch

Quart Verlag has received the support of the
Swiss Federal Office of Culture with a structural
contribution for the years 2016–2020.

Preface
7

Introduction
10

Breathing
12

Surrounded by temperatures
14

Touch
16

Seeing surfaces in the light
18

Hearing in forms and materials
20

Bodies and sizes
22

In balance
24

In movement
26

Temporal rhythms
28

Feeling safe
30

Appendix
33

Preface

There are moments when we are gripped by a location, as we are enveloped by the power of a building or an occasion. Hermann Schmitz describes such situations as a connection between the human body, the space and our emotions.

One memory of being absorbed by spatial conditions in this way stems from my childhood, during wild haymaking, which takes place at altitudes of over 2,000 metres. At that height, there are only few built structures to provide accommodation and protect the hay from the wind and weather. So we had to build *meidas* – the Romansh word for large outdoor haystacks. They were circular, with a diameter of 6 to 8 metres and a height of 6 metres. We often slept in or on a *meida* because it was too far to go home.

Even climbing up it on a ladder required a certain skill. It was a balancing act between the human body and the material. Once we were inside the *meida*, the soft hay surrounded us. Being embedded in this way was a very agreeable and sheltered experience. The smell of the flowers and herbs, the feel of one's own breath and the apparently similar temperature of one's body and the hay – it all led to a strong sense of unison. The moonlight shimmering through the layers of hay also had a transcendent quality, as if connecting us to something beyond our grasp.

The most striking moments were when a thunderstorm swept past and we were forced to shelter beneath some sheeting. The forces of nature felt very near. Often, we felt exposed to the capricious elements, but the confrontation was very lively and rarely threatening. We chose a location for the *meida* that protected it from possible landslides, the wind and the weather. The *meida's* form also made it structurally stable. Those precautions engendered trust.

In such moments, the feeling of experiencing elementary forces can be described as sublime. Sublimity is especially experienced when nature rebels and yet we are not in danger. The distinction between friend and foe seems to be dissolved in such exhilarating moments.

There are other natural experiences I could add to the times in the *meida*: the thunder of rain on a tin roof, or a storm that passes over a protecting cliff face. In such moments, we feel closest to the exuberance of nature and exist in a state of constant interaction with it.

Nature is characterized by repetition and the laws of physics, combined with changes and unique events that are difficult to foresee. However, it is not common to apply the term capricious to it. Bruno Latour points out that it is ultimately impossible to distinguish between natural events and moral judgment. This insight may encourage us to suggest that nature can be moody. We play along with the game, a serious game that defines the relationship between nature and human life.

What can we expect? The resulting relationship with nature would allow us to recognize our own nature, while also letting us discover and develop a broad range of possibilities for our actions. Our own ability, our qualities and those of what we encounter mutually affect each other in an active way. Such a transformation in the relationship between people and things, being open to being touched, allows us to enjoy further experiences.

Recognizing the vibrancy of nature is not a regression to some pre-logical age. It is neither an esoteric claim nor an animist concept, and certainly not an idealization of aesthetics. The aim is simply a direct approach to nature. In this dialectic relationship between realism and idealism, dissonances and conflicts are not uncommon. Resolving them leads to intense partnerships. They also create space for an architecture of proximity – between humans themselves and between humans and things.

In her volume *Bodies in Spaces*, Franziska Wittmann presents the resonance effects between human bodies and their environment. The aim is to observe and appreciate locations that form a protective framework and highlight how we interact with things. We can achieve an awareness of that through physical and sensory experiences in spaces.

Gion A. Caminada, September 2019

Introduction

We breathe the air in a room and smell it, exchanging warmth with our surroundings. We touch the floor, walls and furniture. We see and hear in spaces. Whether stationary or in motion, we exist in relationships of scale with architectural structures. We live in the rhythm of the day and night. And architecture protects our bodies.

Architecture affects us on many levels. As a sequel to the volume *Leistungen der Architektur*, which presents physical phenomena with respect to our use of energy in spaces, this book is aimed at demonstrating the effects of such conditions on humans. Humans and architecture exist in mutual relationships. Human bodies, with their physiology and sensory perceptions, are the focus of attention. I wish to create an awareness of physical and sensory phenomena in spaces, which always affect us in houses, including their interconnections. Bodies are in a constant state of exchange with their surroundings. Tiny differences in energy lead to a resonance effect.

A cold handrail draws heat from my body, direct light can be dazzling, the smell of wooden walls is enveloping; I need all my weight to open a heavy door or a mere arm movement for light sliding doors; steps echo on marble flooring, voices beneath vaults ...

Architecture involves sensations. In a resonant environment, we feel ourselves more, and also more consciously. By touching a wall – made either of rough or smooth plaster, soft textile or hard stone – we also feel our hands.

Spatial sensations combine to form a complex experience of and in architecture, with diverse interrelationships. Gardens, baths, cellars, churches and concert halls create clearly felt stimuli. Rounded edges, light reflections on porous stone and a finely scattered reverberation on reliefs make subtle phenomena tangible. Stimuli, both large and very small, make us resonate in an atmosphere that is more than a sense of comfort, since its evenness is more tiring than buoyant.

This collection of physiological laws, architectural consequences, examples and quotes presents spatial moments in which bodies and architecture exist in conscious interrelationships. The book demonstrates opportunities for designing and living, while also giving space to sensitivities, allowing one to dream of spaces that support, involve and touch us: spaces that we love.

Breathing

Air at locations
Air pressure decreases with increasing altitude and depends on the weather and temperature.

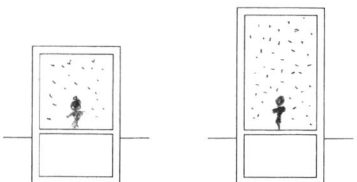

Air in room sizes
Larger room volumes contain more air.

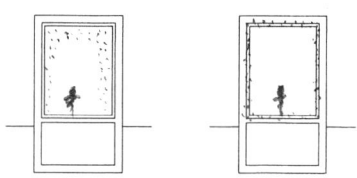

Air and materials
Materials emit odours in the room and absorb varying amounts of odours from the room, depending on their qualities.

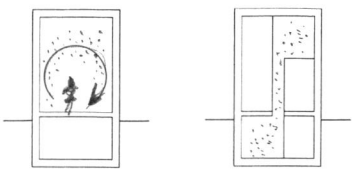

Air in motion
Circulation cools the skin and unsettles dust, which is then perceived as aridity in people's respiratory tracts. Spatial passages – especially vertical access routes – carry odours to adjoining rooms.

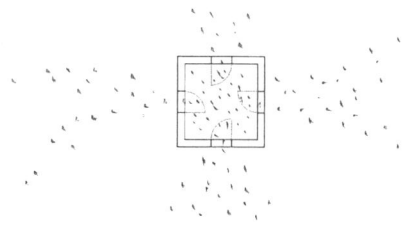

Opening and closing
Opening windows enables the exchange of air and enhances the oxygen content of the interior air, while reducing odours. The quality of a room's air depends on the quality of the outdoor air.

Breathing exchanges air between bodies and spaces. Air flows through the mouth or nose into bodies and, after being filtered and warmed, reaches the lungs. Oxygen is passed on to the blood vessels via the lungs' membrane. Exhaling removes humidity from the lungs and ejects carbon dioxide. Breathing allows us to perceive scents. When inhaling, smells are passed via the upper nasal cavity and olfactory mucosa on to the brain by chemoreceptors. Scents affect our emotions and our nervous, hormone and immune systems. The longer a scent lingers, the weaker its perception becomes. Smells are remembered longer than other forms of sensory perception.

Alvar Aalto, Paimio Sanatorium, Finland, 1933. [Fig. 3]

The Paimio Sanatorium is situated in a forest. Air and light – non-dazzling when reclining and sunny on the balconies and terraces – are aimed at supporting the healing process in the building.

Alvar Aalto, Studio, Helsinki, Finland, 1955. [Fig. 4]

The springy chairs in Aalto's Paimio Sanatorium lean backwards to aid breathing.
In the hollow, dynamic space in his Helsinki studio, air moves from the garden through the windows at various levels and on through the adjoining rooms.

Oxygen and room height.

«Previous investigations have shown that the CO_2 concentration does not increase uniformly in the room. It acts much more like warm air, concentrating primarily at ceiling level.»
Junghans, in: Eberle/Aicher, p. 51

Fragrant linden tree courtyard in early summer, Zurich, Switzerland. [Fig. 5]

«Cities have a smell of their own, which is influenced by the geographical position, by the climate, by the way of living in them: the location by the sea, by a lagoon, high in the mountains, in the desert.» Frank, in: Spatial Expeditions, p. 45

Event.

Events – individual or recurrent – affect the odour of rooms, for instance in kitchens or workshops. Odours can define the relationship between us and the room, the time of day, the day of the week or festive occasions.

Theophil von Hansen, Great Hall of the Musikverein, Vienna, Austria, 1870. [Fig. 1]

Acoustics are created out of the space – the materials in their form – and the audience. The space also has its own odour. «In the great hall, the scent of the rosewood and palisander still dominate today.» Metzger, p. 41 [trans.]

P. Zumthor, Swiss Pavilion, Hanover Expo, 2000.

«The Swiss Pavilion is an olfactory event that one remembers, because scents are unconsciously taken in together with a location and remembered for a very long time.» Blaser, p. 9 [trans.]

«The stacked walls consist of solid, untreated larch or Douglas fir wood that is joined in openly visible structures. The biological mass has a scent, shrinking or swelling under the influence of weather [...].» Hönig, p. 105 [trans.]

Gion A. Caminada, Terrihütte, Greina, Switzerland, 2007. [Fig. 2]

The window at the head end allows air to flow into the room at the level of the people lying there.

Peace.

«The sense of smell was solicited primarily to accommodate the wish for repose. The approaches to the house and to the bedroom [...] called for plants with odoriferous flowers or foliage in the vicinity.» Corbin, p. 80

Surrounded by temperatures

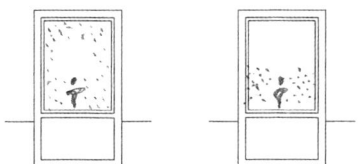

Radiation exchange between bodies
All surfaces – the skin and surfaces in the room –
exchange radiation. Warm surfaces emit heat, while
cold surfaces absorb heat. Heat radiation is warming
regardless of the air temperature, and needs no air
movement.

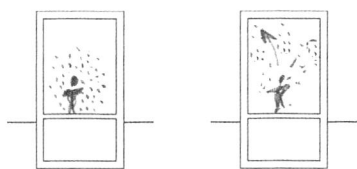

Warm air and cooling air movement
Warm air warms us, while a flow of air over the skin draws
moisture from the body and is cooling.

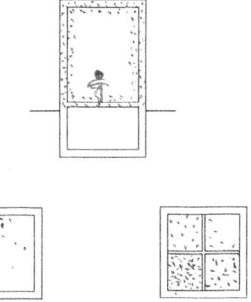

Spatial heat
Warm floors, walls or ceilings
envelope bodies with their temperature.
A source of heat at a specific location creates
heat hierarchies within a space.
Rooms with different temperatures provide choices.

Exterior spaces
Balconies are either warming or cooling places depending on
their orientation towards the sun, their position in or in front
of the façade, and the form and material of the balustrade.

Temperatures are perceived through the skin – by touching a material, as air moving past or as heat radiation. Thermoreceptors on the skin combine with nerves in the brain to act as heat regulators. Moving air and higher humidity make higher temperatures bearable. Smaller heating or cooling events only fleetingly lead to a sense of warmth or cold, after which the sensation becomes neutral and the stimulus is adapted. Evenly warm temperatures are tiring, while temperature changes have an invigorating effect.

Kohler und Partner, apartment renovation in Bern, Switzerland, 2004. [Fig. 8]

«Warmth can have such different qualities: radiant heat [...] can be bearable even in summer, but even in cold winter warm air heating is unpleasant.» Day, p. 49

«The wall position of a fireplace introduces the habit of sitting in front of the fire, replacing the older social figure of lying or crouching around a central hearth.» Selle, p. 96 [trans.]

This seating niche in front of a fire attempts to give warmth its own space.

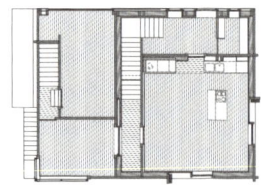

Gion A. Caminada, Segmüller House, Vignon, Switzerland, 2001. [Fig. 10]

«The interior is designed in a way that alternates between cold and warm rooms. Like traditional farmhouses, the route leads to the next living room via the unheated staircase.» Sonderegger, p. 17 [trans.]

Valerio Olgiati, House K+N, Wollerau, Switzerland, 2005. [Fig. 9]

The ground floor can be opened in four directions. Sliding windows disappear into the ground. The room becomes a pavilion in the garden, creating low-level views of the exterior – on three sides into the nearby surroundings and on one side into the distance over Lake Zurich.

Wind.

«For instance the light ringing of a wind chime in traditional Japanese gardens evokes the refreshing effect of a gust of wind on the skin, even before we can actually feel it.» Schütz, in: Gantenbein/Rodewald, p. 64 [trans.]

Peter Zumthor, Luzi House, Jenaz, Switzerland, 2002.
« Living in a blockhouse of solid wood has a special quality which is felt both in its aura and in the physical experience of living there. As opposed to stone or concrete, logs do not draw off warmth from the human body, and thus even in cold weather they feel warm. Conversely, when it is warm or hot, the wooden beams do not radiate previously absorbed heat as stone or metal would, and so their effect is actually cooling.»
Zumthor/Durisch (ed.), Volume 2, p. 133

B. Hoffmann, C. Kahleyss, Leya Wingback Chair, for Freifrau, 2014. [Fig. 6]

Wingback chairs provide a shell for bodies to recline in. The head can rest and the sensitive neck area is protected from draughts and radiative cooling.

Sunny balcony and shade in the garden. [Fig. 7]

«She felt the morning air cooling her eyelids and cheeks. The sun glimmered in the redcurrant bushes by the fence, while the rest of the garden still remained shady. Fanny held her warm cup of coffee in both hands and strolled among the beds.» Freudenthaler, p. 67 [trans.]

Touch

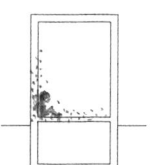

Materials conduct body heat
Heavy, smooth materials conduct more heat than light, porous materials.

Pressure of forms
Edges and corners are tangible as pressure or pain. The surfaces of materials are smooth or coarse and have a specific texture, rigidity or elasticity, viscosity and consistency.

Things have mass
Carrying things makes their weight perceptible.

The skin – which has a large surface and is permeable – senses touch, vibrations, temperatures, pressure and pain. Thermal and pain receptors react very quickly, while haptic and tactile perception takes longer. The active haptic stimuli threshold is much more sensitive than passive tactile perception. The most sensitive parts of the body are the lips, fingertips and fingernails. Supplementary information is provided by muscles and joints – in movement and in relation to gravity.

Alvar Aalto, Villa Mairea, Noormarkku, Finland, 1937. [Fig. 13]
The sections of the columns enveloped in rattan are less hard and cold. Hard flooring and soft carpets alternate.
«Gravity is measured by the bottom of the foot; we trace the density and texture of the ground through our soles.»
Pallasmaa, p. 62

Hans J. Wegner, Papa Bear Chair, for A.P.Stolen, 1951.
«[...] the armrests have been cut free from the seat, so the sitter can turn freely in the chair. The Papa Bear Chair's claws – made from pieces of wood – have a number of functions: they prevent the sitter's hands from soiling the fabric when rising and hide the joinery beneath the fabric.»
Holmsted Olesen, p. 208

Carrying. [Fig. 16]
A chair with an additional backrest bar can be carried with one hand. The lower the bar, the easier it is to carry.

Klemens Grund, Kitchen table, 2017. [Fig. 14]
Rounded edges make it possible to touch tabletop corners and table legs with one's hands and feet.

M. Lipparini, Basket, for Bonaldo, 2013. [Fig. 15]
The bed allows one to lean against it while sitting up. Like a wing chair, it also protects the head and neck, giving one a spatial sense of security.

Touching the floor.

«Beneath him, in the choir, the devout are throwing themselves down upon countless carpets. They are kneeling, touching the floor with their foreheads [...].» Énard, p. 37 [trans.]

«[...] and we also hear with our knees and the soles of our feet. That ist why Oriental carpets with their lively ornamentation are not just pleasing to our eyes but also have important acoustic functions for the room as well as for our bodies – which should be one and the same. Carpets are meant to be walked on with bare feet, and it is via the soles of our feet that their quiet and tranquility enters our body. We hear with our entire body.»
Conrads/Leitner, p. 30

Alvar Aalto, Villa Mairea, Noormarkku, Finland, 1937. [Fig. 11]

«The door pull is the handshake of a building.» Pallasmaa, p. 67

Emanuel de Witte, Interior with woman at the piano, 1665/70. [Fig. 12]

«The rooms form a linear alignment without creating the impression of threatening depth. [...] The bed stands in a corner of the room behind the door; the carpet lies in front of the bed so that people getting up do not need to stand on the cold stone floor with their bare feet. [...] The table and chairs stand directly by the window, where it is brightest. And what light floods the room! The distribution of light and shadow emphasises the depth, highlights the distance and stresses the physical, material reality of the room.»
Rybczynski, p. 75 f. [trans.]

Seeing surfaces in the light

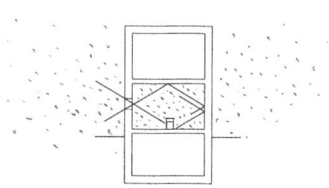

Light intensity and colours
Direct and reflected light create
brightness and colours in the room.
Too much brightness and too much contrast
between surface brightnesses are dazzling.
Things are seen horizontally at eye level or from above.

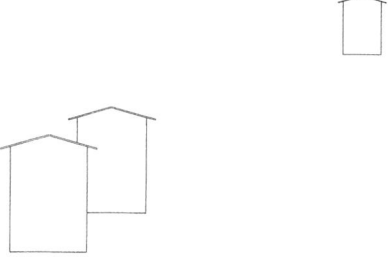

Distances and perspective
Sight measures distances within the horizon. Perspective
makes distant things appear smaller and lighter than
closer things. In dry air, distant things appear to be
closer. Things in front conceal things behind them.

Visual perception
Dark things appear to be smaller than light things.
Light things beside dark things make the dark things
appear even darker.

Details
Sight drifts, jumps and stops at details.

When light reaches the eye, it is processed by ganglion cells. The information is passed on to the brain via optic nerve strands, where visual perception takes place. The eye attempts to perceive surfaces as coherent elements. Our eyes, head and body are moveable, enabling serial images. Physiologically, we see colours and different levels of brightness. Light adaptation occurs much faster than dark adaptation.

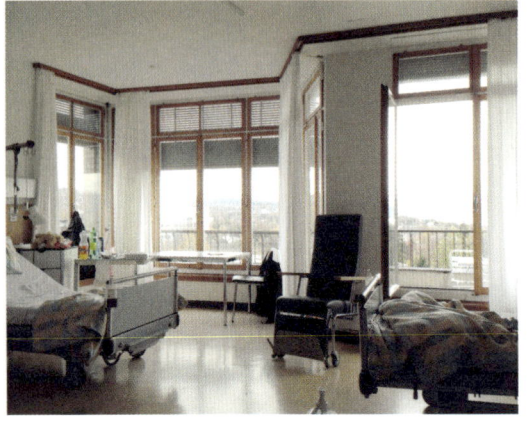

Haefeli Moser Steiger, Zurich University Hospital, Switzerland, 1953. [Fig. 19]

The spatial façade creates places with light from three sides and views in three directions. The room opens up and yet the height of the window sills has a retaining effect. One can step out and can open the windows – actively inhabiting the space and moving from the inside to the outside. Spaces merge into one another without losing a sense of envelopment. Light is reflected on the floor. The ceiling is matt and does not dazzle people when reclining.

Louis Sullivan, Bayard Building, New York, USA, 1899. [Fig. 22]

Details give the eyes a similar density of information from various distances.

RCR Architectes, Athletics stadium, Olot, Spain, from 1991. [Figs. 20,21]

The running track seeks the colour of the surroundings. The topography enables seating formed out of concrete elements. Runners appear and disappear behind hills and trees.

Forest.

Coolness, odours, sounds, movements and green semi-darkness make the forest a place of physical regeneration.

«Things are entirely recognizable in their forms; it is rather the obstruction of vision by things themselves, by the tree-trunks and bushes, the branches and leaves, which enclose us in their own realm, almost as if in a kind of inner space.» Bollnow, p. 205

Seeing distances.

«At three or four stories […] you can see details in the street – the people, their faces, foliage, shops.»
«A person's face is just recognizable at about 70 feet.»
Alexander, p. 118 / p. 312

Room ceiling.
Painted room ceilings (in entrances) inspire one to stop, raise one's head and look up.

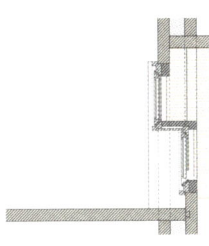

Gion A. Caminada, Stiva da morts, Vrin, Switzerland, 2002. [Fig. 17]
The deep window soffits allow people to show or conceal themselves in specific perspectives.

Luis Barragan, B. Meyer House, Mexiko City, 1981. [Fig. 18]
The grid between interior and exterior spaces allows one to see from the dark into the light – during the day from inside outwards.

Olafur Eliasson, Your colour memory, 2004.
«At an interval of 30 seconds, one primary colour switches to another, so after 15 seconds, the respective mixed colours of yellow, cyan and magenta are created. In our subjective colour perception, afterimages in complementary colours appear with a delay of 10-15 seconds, before disappearing after another 10-15 seconds. In this way, our colour perception constantly changes until it increasingly fades due to the complexity. In a dark side-room that visitors can enter from the oval, visitors can see nothing except afterimages they have brought with them from the main room. The viewers are not only recipients, but also creators of the light phenomena.»
Frank, p. 149 [trans.]

Hosokawa Katsumoto, Hojo-Teien Zen garden, Japan, 15th century.
Stones lie in groups on a gravel surface. It is impossible to see all stones from a single perspective. «When sitting at a specific place outside the garden, which one cannot enter, one witnesses a presented ellipse that is created by the arrangement of the stones. To the observer from a specific perspective, the garden becomes complete. This also means there are specific viewpoints from where one does not feel included, where the garden remains a fragment.»
Pöppel, p. 200 ff. [trans.]

Colours.
«When people are exposed for a long time to blue light, their blood pressure changes. The pulse slows down and their blood sugar levels fall because blue light affects the pancreas. [...] Colours have an effect, not only blue and not only through the eyes. They are oscillating, flowing, living energy, precisely measurable physical values.»
Wansch, p. 236 [trans.]

Hearing in forms and materials

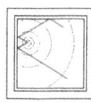

Spatial sound
Sound spreads in all directions, reflects off surfaces –
materials and their structures – and surrounds us
from all directions as spatial sound.
We perceive the distance of the sound source,
as well as its tone and intensity.

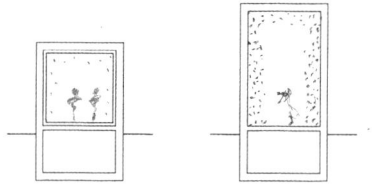

Tones through language and music
The temporal difference between direct sound
and its echo creates spatial sound.
Language is easier to understand in rooms with a short
echo. Music develops in rooms with specific acoustics –
and is more sonorous in spaces with longer echoes.

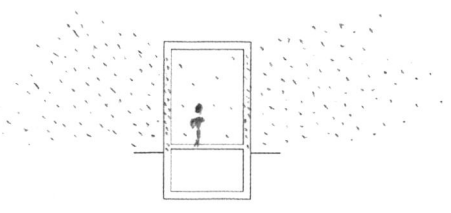

Sound and noise
The louder the surroundings, the more important
sound insulation becomes for rooms.

When perceiving sounds, the body is stimulated by oscillation. Not only the ears perceive sounds. The entire body senses sounds as vibrations in different intensities – the chest and stomach more than arms and legs. Ears can locate a source of sound, above all by calculating the different information from both ears. Our hearing sense reacts more sensitively to reflections from the side than from a frontal or vertical direction. The direction of the first sound signal – direct sound or its first reflection – is presumed to be the source of the sound.

Herzog & de Meuron, design for a fountain at Marktplatz in Basel, Switzerland, 1985. [Fig. 25]

«Herzog & de Meuron suggested a lancet-shaped indentation placed into the middle rosette and covered with a grid. A double-walled resonance volume leads from it down to the Birsig canal and, like an ear, makes the gushing of the river audible.»

Mack, p. 25

Treading on materials. [Fig. 26]
Dead leaves make walking audible.

Squares.
«[...] and under typical urban noise conditions, a loud voice can just barely be heard across 70 feet. This may mean that people feel half-consciously tied together in plazas that have diameters of 70 feet or less.»

Alexander, p. 312 f.

Sounds of bodies in spaces.
«It is already difficult to verbalize our feeling of the height of a room. [...] and besides, why should we need rooms of different heights. [...] But there is something else we must say in this context: it is not enough to look – one also has to listen: after all, the various heights ‹speak› to us. The power of acoustics has its roots in the way which ties a person into the sound of a room, into the particular time of a room. Yet it is man himself who must make the room resound – with his steps, his speech, with any activity that generates sounds, even with his breathing. This interconnection between man and space, which is achieved with sounds and affects even our innermost being, is like a kind of dialogue which is determined by the acoustic premises. This dialogue enables us to experience ourselves in the sound of a room.»

Conrads/Leitner, p. 29

Height.
«From three stories you can yell out, and catch the attention of someone below. Above four stories these connections break down.»

Alexander, p. 118

Herzog & de Meuron,
Elbphilharmonie Hamburg,
Germany, 2016. [Fig. 23]

Music spreads in all directions. Applause returns from all sides.

Peter Zumthor, Swiss Pavilion,
Expo Hanover, Germany, 2000.

«The performance also involves the sounds and noises of the bar. They include clinking glasses, clattering plates and the hissing of the coffee machine. The till makes electronic chirping sounds, the coffee piston bangs on the powder receptacle and the lid of the dishwasher slots into place. The blade of the slicing machine sings, refrigerator draws rumble when closed and the coffee grinder whirrs. The telephone rings, trays slide on their racks, taps gurgle and small change rattles in the till. [...]

Almost 350 musicians play in the pavilion during the entire duration of the exhibition. They make the resonating body sound according to a concept by the composer Daniel Ott. Yet not only the composed and improvised tones, but also the everyday sounds of the pavilion are part of the living sound installation, part of the performance.»

Hönig, p. 131 [trans.]

Romero Schaefle Architekten, Vogt Landschaftsarchitekten, Hotel Greulich, Zurich, Switzerland, 2003. [Fig. 24]

The city, people and birch trees create the sounds in the inner courtyard. «Our steps reveal the acoustic wealth of the location: first we hear the wooden jetty, then a short stretch on gravel, a few steps on iron and then the slowly receding echo of the glass roof gable. [...] The small copse and the glass-covered courtyard form an urban arena with three interleaving, ideally coordinated spatial sequences. The central glass body serves as a resonator and a reflector. Various highly staggered roofs and numerous balconies articulate the overall sound space. Four courtyard drives act as sound lenses to the outside city.»

Bürgin/Maag, in: Stadtklang, p. 72 [trans.]

Bodies and sizes

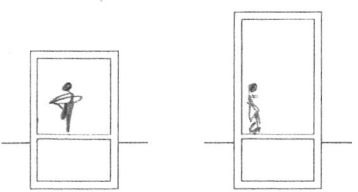

Proportions
Humans and spaces exist in a mutual relationship –
depending on sizes and geometries perceived from one's
own position in spaces – at their centre or
at their edges.

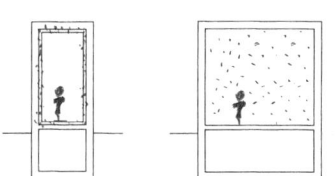

Spatial sizes
In small spaces, materials are nearby, present and have a
direct effect on the body. In large volumes, walls are far
away from human bodies.

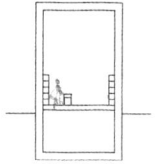

Bodies and things in spaces
Lying, sitting, kneeling, standing and in movement,
people occupy spaces between walls and furniture.
Things are within reach or further away.

Proprioception is the perception of one's own body – its size, the relationships between its individual parts and its position and movement in space. A human body's size is described as its size in a standing position, measured from the sole of its feet to the forehead. The span of one's arms from middle finger to middle finger is approximately the same as one's body size.

Tatami mat.
With their proportions of 1:2, tatami mats allow a range of combinations. One mat has the size of one sleeping space.

Writing desk.
Sitting with one's back to a bookshelf allows one to ‹fall back on› something from the desk.

Ulna and foot.
«[The builder] established order by measuring. In order to measure he took his pace, his foot, his forearm, or his finger. By imposing the order of his foot or his arm, he created a module that regulates the entire work.»
Le Corbusier, p. 134

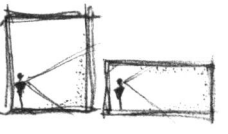

Quiescence and room size. [Fig. 30]
In a room with high ceilings, the walls are initially in the line of view. In a room with low ceilings, the ceiling is visible in a person's quiescent view. High-ceilinged rooms reveal the ceilings and floors after moving one's head and eyes upwards.

Frankfurt kitchen. [Fig. 29]
«The environment comes close to the body's space, the hand becomes the most important organ of orientation, the body sits on an office chair with wheels or stands almost motionless in rationalised, minimal movement. Accordingly, spatial perception must shrink into a capsule; the spatial subtraction reduces the effort required to achieve orientation.»
Selle, p. 66 [trans.]

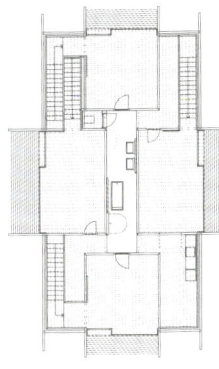

Peter Zumthor, Luzi House, Jenaz, Switzerland, 2002. [Fig. 27]

The way from the bedroom to the staircase is broader – to allow a lying human body to be carried out of it.

St. Peter Mistail, Alvaschein, Switzerland, around 800. [Fig. 28]

Spaces, people and the painted, almost room-high figure exist in a relationship of scales.

Sizes.

«This is one of the original themes of architecture: the relationship between mathematical precision and physical presents, between human feelings and natural imperfection. Proportions, representing the correct relationships of scale, form a system in and for itself. It requires special effort to relate this ideal quality to ourselves. It appears to pay special attention to our physicality. Our perception is not limited to a front view of static images in the distance. And even there, a lying rectangle has a completely different effect on us than a standing object with the same proportions, not to mention a diagonal one. Furthermore, our eye level can only be changed to a very modest degree, our arm span is limited and we can only grasp what fits in our hands. Sizes are also important, not just size relationships.»

Tschanz, in Gerber/Joanelly/Franck, p. 37 f. [trans.]

Doors and corridors.

People walk through narrow doors individually, one after another. Broad doors allow them to walk beside each other. Low doors force them to bend over – if there is also a threshold, the door is perceived as a hole that needs to be climbed through, which avoids bumping one's head. Like doors, corridors allow a different number of people to walk beside each other depending on their width.

In balance

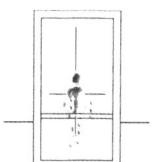

Equilibrium and directions
Orientation in space includes perceiving the effect of gravity. Top and bottom, front and back, right and left are experienced as directions in relation to the body.

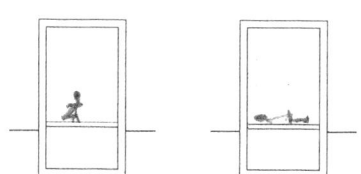

Standing and lying down
Being vertical in a space makes us experience a different space from being horizontal in the space.

The sense of balance consists of several senses – perception of gravity and acceleration, orientation and inclination, as well as touch and depth sensitivity. Perception of gravity has its centre in the equilibrium organ in the inner ear and the cerebellum. The information from different systems is combined and forwarded to the arm and leg muscles.

Midday light in Mistail, Alvaschein, Switzerland, around 800. [Fig. 32]

«We all know the sacred space where we automatically assume an adequate posture, even if we are not familiar with the liturgical significance of the building forms. And we all know the impressive, prestigious spaces in which we nevertheless remain relaxed [...].»
Franck/Franck, p. 190 [trans.]

Symmetry.

«Symmetries are something we react to intuitively and with great sensitivity. [...] Our sense of balance lies in all the senses together. It above all combines the modalities of external perception with the body's own self-awareness. Standing upright and moving forwards in balance are a dynamic application and continuation of the symmetrical body structure.»
Franck/Franck, p. 220 [trans.]

Furniture between bodies and the floor.

Stools with three legs or ones close to each other are more likely to tip over than stools with four legs or legs spaced further apart. Tables with three legs never wobble on an even surface. Four legs require a very precisely even floor.

Gravitation.

«The head so heavy. [...] Fanny wanted to let her head fall onto the tabletop, onto her forehead. Her head would then continue to fall, onto one side, onto a cheek. Fanny would lie with her head on the tabletop and no longer move. Her arms would hang beneath the table. [...] Each time when she experienced one of those moments, Fanny thought her head and upper body really were about to fall on the table. This time, she would be unable to remain seated.» Freudenthaler, p. 22 [trans.]

Bodies in geometrical spaces.
«The perception of external space, the dimensions of the vertical and horizontal and the third dimension, distance, is an accompaniment of the fact of body posture and eqilibrium […].»
Gibson, p. 72

Lying, sitting, standing up in spaces.
«[The] person lying in bed has a different relationship with space, or rather, he has a different space from one who is moving in an upright posture.» Bollnow, p. 163 f. When seated, mainly the rear side of the body is in contact with something. «Standing is not a position that, once assumed, can be maintained for a long period. Instead, there is always an endangered condition of balance between gravity and steadfastness, between the body and the world, that must constantly be reattained and actively upheld.» Eickhoff, p. 127 [trans.]

Gion A. Caminada, Tierparkturm, Goldau, Switzerland, 2017. [Fig. 31]
The boards mounted diagonally with respect to the floor allow lateral light to be reflected inside and irritate one's sense of balance.

In movement

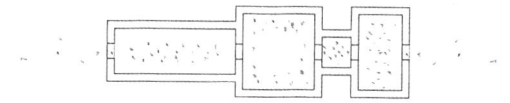

Narrowness and breadth
When moving through spaces, their size and form become perceptible, as well as the sequence of narrow and broad spaces.

Stairs and ramps
Stairs and ramps connect heights – more slowly or quickly depending on their steepness. Platforms slow people down. When moving on stairs, their measure is perceived as a repetition after the first few steps. We can sense the smallest changes in the stairs as we move along them.

Opening doors and windows.
A door that opens outwards requires us to step back on arrival.
We can use our body weight to lean against doors that open inwards. A heavy gate needs our entire body weight, while a light sliding door simply requires an arm movement.
To open windows outwards, we must lean out, while opening inwards requires a step backwards – backwards and sideways for single-leaf windows, straight backwards for double-leaf windows.

Our sense of movement is based on receptors in our joints, muscles and sinews. A muscle moves the body by contracting and relaxing. Movements differ with respect to force, speed and precision, thereby requiring more or less effort and energy. Gravity, muscle power and centrifugal forces create movement.

Grafton, University Campus UTEC Lima, Peru, 2015. [Fig. 35]

The building is designed as a topography that is open to the city and connected to it by a ramp. The movement through the building communicates great freedom. The broad entrances allow people to stroll, linger, wander, stand still and have conversations on their way.

Walkways in housing.

«A room that can be traversed in one or two steps gives an entirely different experience from a room requiring fifteen or twenty steps. A room with a ceiling you can touch is quite different from one with a ceiling eleven feet high.» Hall, p. 54

We can look through an enfilade as we walk from room to room. Apartments that allow one to walk in a circuit have an open end to the movement through the space.

Treading on surfaces.

«Footwear and its space-creating function are so fascinating precisely because walking is such a basic and common way of ‹apprehending› space. Shoes as sound instruments which, not unlike hard wooden, leather or felt covered drumsticks, strike a hard or soft floor, a cobblestone pavement or a polished granite surface. Steps activate space. Footwear as percussive instrument. It is through the act of walking around in a room that its specific sound is first made audible.»
Conrads/Leitner, p. 32

Through gardens.

Cloisters can be meditative or reflective places. Stepping stones in the ponds of Japanese gardens make us concentrate on our steps.

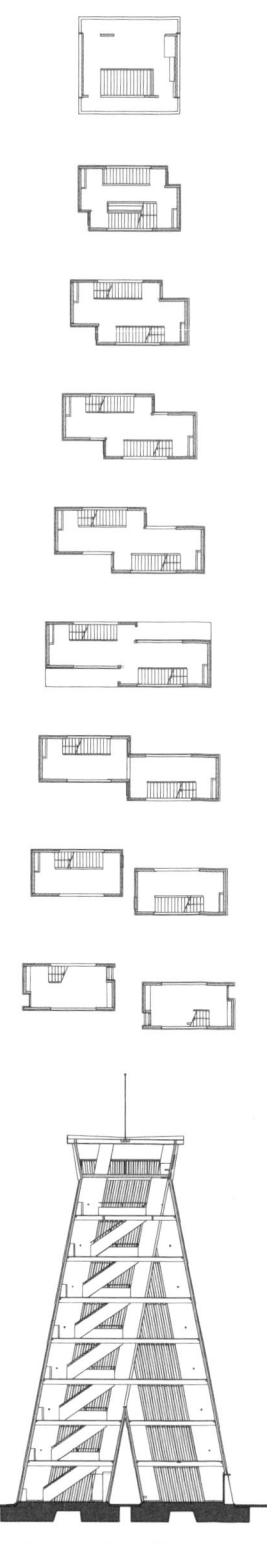

Gion A. Caminada, Tierparkturm, Goldau, Switzerland, 2016. [Fig. 36]

The tower is part of the paths through the park. Two stairs connect the ground, a central platform and the viewing platform at the top.

Lois Welzenbacher, Mimi Settari House, Briol, Italy, 1923. [Figs. 33,34]
A curved path leads to the house. «The wall leads us around the corner – we have not voluntarily decided to turn at right angles to our present course. We follow the wall – its continuation and also its quality therefore determine the way we walk, influence the way we feel beside it. While we walk along it, we are confronted by its impression.» Jäkel, p. 56 [trans.] «The different routes the residents need to take in this house can be imagined as a constant exchange between centrifugal and centripetal forces, which however always relate back to the centre of the building.» Jäkel, p. 51 [trans.]

Herzog & de Meuron, Prada Tokyo, Japan, 2003.
Highly polished flooring and soft carpets alternate. The carpets slow people down – the deeper the pile, the greater the effect.

English garden.
«In Munich, one can observe how joggers, cyclists, horse-riders and pedestrians map out the park as a space and encounter each other on their way. It is a grand tableau, a living image of simultaneous appropriation movements. Everything occurs at once and yet for itself, at differing speeds.»
Selle, in: Hauskeller, p. 277 f. [trans.]

Temporal rhythms

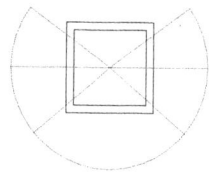

Light
Light and shade in a room create a framework
for living during the day.
Darkness and silence frame the night.

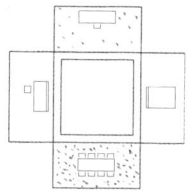

Living as the day passes
Rooms have a relationship to directions.
Living can be connected to the changing
position of the sun.

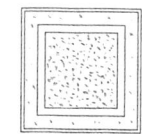

Seasons in rooms
Furnishing can mean changing sizes and
materials according to the season.

We live between the sky and the earth on a planet rotating around the sun and around its own axis. This dictates the rhythms of annual and daily life. The circadian rhythm has a period length of around 24 hours and helps the body to live according to repetitive phenomena. It influences the heart frequency, the sleep-wake rhythm, blood pressure, hormone levels and body temperature. The most important rhythm and measure of time is the alternating light intensity of the atmosphere.

Morning light. [Figs. 40,41]
The rising sun (direct light) and the light of the full moon (reflected light) at dawn between buidlings.

St. Stephen's Cathedral,
Vienna, Austria.
The church is orientated towards the sunrise on December 26, 1137. Every December 26 – St. Stephen's Day – the first rays of morning light shine into the centre of the church, from the eastern window to the western gate.

Space and time.
«I have always known that architecture was determined by the hour and the event; and it was this hour that I sought in vain, confusing it with nostalgia, the countryside, summer: it was an hour of suspension, the mythical *cinco del la tarde* of Seville, but also the hour of the railroad timetable, of the end of the lesson, of dawn.»
Rossi, p. 80

Light and colours.
«The slogan of the competition for which it was designed was ‹the blue of the sky›, and now when I look at those huge, blue, sheet-metal roofs, so sensitive to day and evening light as well as to that of the seasons, they sometimes seem deep blue, sometimes the clearest azure. The pink stucco of the walls covers the Emilian brick of the old cemetery, and it too displays the effects of the light, appearing almost white or else dark pink.»
Rossi, p. 15

Seasons. [Figs. 42,43]
«We are embedded in the way of the world, we are connected to this world and even synchronised with it; the garden is a place that makes this visually clear and tangible to us.»
Pöppel, p. 170 [trans.]

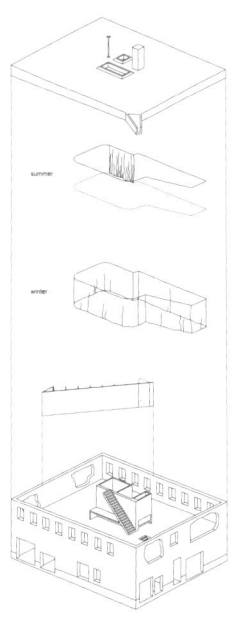 

Arno Brandlhuber, Antivilla, Krampnitz, Germany, 2015. [Figs. 37,38]
A curtain divides the open floor plan: in winter, it creates a room around the warm core, and in the summer, one around the northern sleeping area.

At home.
«Here we know the daily path of the sun, when it shines in January and when in July in this part of the world, from where and into which window at midsummer the desired breeze begins to blow at six in the afternoon and in which weather conditions swarms of stinging flies suddenly appear.»
Neutra, Mensch und Wohnen, life and human habitat, p. 21 [trans.]

Gion A. Caminada, Casa Caminada, Fürstenau, Switzerland, 2018. [Fig. 39]
«Architecture creates inner, outer and interim spaces that allow different resonances as interactions between states of liveliness. Qualities in housing occur when architecture manages not to isolate its inhabitants from the phenomena of nature, instead creating a relationship to them. I do not mean returning to climatically hard living, but a type of living that goes beyond the superficial contemporary notion of comfort and allows different temperatures and light intensities, denser and less dense rooms, muffled and sonorous acoustics, thereby finding qualities that fulfil our bodies' need for a continuous, altering exchange with the environment.»
Wittmann, in: werk 7/8, 2018 [trans.]

Feeling safe

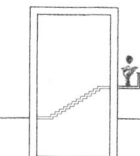

Not falling over
Floors are more or less smooth.
Stairs should be evenly steep.
Railings and balustrades or horizontal supports
provide protection from different height levels.

Orientation in rooms
Structures with different sizes, changing light
conditions and perceptive stimuli aid orientation.
Perceiving spatial boundaries creates
a sense of security.

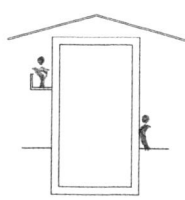

Protection against the elements
The envelope of a house distinguishes between the
inside and outside. It creates interior, exterior and
interim spaces – as well as various relationships
to the weather.

Fire
Non-flammable materials and fire-resistant apertures
stop fires from spreading. Free-standing houses must
keep a distance from each other. Fire compartments
provide protection in buildings.
Short walkways allow people to leave
the building quickly.

Physical security is perceptible as a state where no physical danger can be assumed. Houses primarily fulfil the need for security. They can also create a sense of comfort.

Carlo Scarpa, Fondazione Querini Stampalia, Venice, Italy, 1963. [Figs. 46,47]

The ground floor and garden of a library building allow floodwater to enter the space. The base and drainage channels in the floor protect the house. Steps and elevated walkways allow people to walk through the building without getting their feet wet.

Sacred buildings.

«And above all, shield the approach to the [sacred] site, so that it can only be approached on foot, and through a series of gateways and thresholds which reveal it gradually.»

Alexander, p. 134

Valerio Olgiati, Villa Além, Briol, Portugal, 2014. [Fig. 48]

«In our house, the bedrooms […] have no visual relationship to the outside world and the rooms only receive light from above. The impression of being underground creates a strong sense of security. […] The path to them through a semi-circular hall that is only lit from above has a disorientating effect. One therefore feels that the bedrooms are removed from the other rooms in the building and far away from the outside environment.»

Olgiati, in: archithese 4, 2015, p. 38 [trans.]

Jaeger Koechlin, Friedli House, Bern, Switzerland, 2017. [Fig. 49]

The roof creates a covered exterior space that protects people from the rain. It in turn projects to cover a seating area in the garden. Railings secure height differences. Shutters are closed at night.

Momentum.

«Just as Fanny had earlier wanted to let her head drop on the tabletop, so she now had the feeling of sinking into the ground. She stood at the edge and swayed, as if she were about to fall backwards […]» Freudenthaler, p. 67 [trans.]

Ernst Gisel, Blue Studio, Zurich, Switzerland, 1973. [Fig. 44]

«The blue studio is hidden in the southern corner of the almost rectangular plot [...]. The reserved nature of the studio building is further enhanced by the wall surrounding the courtyard, shielding it from the access road. Likewise, the tall, blue-painted, roughly plastered front wall is almost entirely closed on the upper level.»

Maurer/Oechselin, p. 194 [trans.]

Peter Zumthor, Klangkörper, Expo Hanover, Germany, 2000.

«The inside of the sound body initially appears to be labyrinthine. It has a textile-like structure without any continuous passageways or corridors, which are classic elements of architectural orientation in a building. So there is no fixed guidance and one wonders through the passages and courtyards, seeking one's own way as if in a forest. However, the sound body is not a maze because it lacks two qualities: it does not seem to be inescapable, nor does it have a centre. Apart from at four places, with a size of only a few square metres, one looks directly outwards from every point inside the pavilion.»

Hönig, p. 147 f. [trans.]

Walking.

Brickwork steps, stairs with seating-steps and rungs with greater tread surfaces while walking upwards, boards with good grip, a footpath with a certain height difference compared to the road – all these aspects can provide greater security.

Hans Döllgast, Alter Südfriedhof, Munich, Germany, 1954. [Fig. 45]

Fine steel columns support the new roof, creating a covered exterior area that protects people from the rain.

Credits

Breathing
1 Musikverein Wien
2 Lucia Degonda
3, 4 © Pieter Lozie
5 Franziska Wittmann

Surrounded by temperatures
6 Freifrau Sitzmöbelmanufaktur
7 Franziska Wittmann
8 Hanna Kohler
9 © Archive Olgiati
10 Gion A. Caminada

Touch
11 Åke E:son Lindman
12 Museum Boijmans Van Beuningen
13 Åke E:son Lindman
14 Klemens Grund
15 Bonaldo
16 Franziska Wittmann

Seeing surfaces in the light
17 Gion A. Caminada
18 © Barragan Foundation /
    2019, ProLitteris, Zurich
19 Silvan Blumenthal
20, 21 Hisao Suzuki
22 © Vanni Archive / Art Resource, NY

Hearing in forms and materials
23 © Michael Zapf
24 © Christian Vogt
25 © Herzog & de Meuron
26 Franziska Wittmann

Bodies and sizes
27 Atelier Peter Zumthor
28 Franziska Wittmann
29 Das neue Frankfurt, 5/1926-27
30 Franziska Wittmann

In balance
31 Gion A. Caminada
32 Franziska Wittmann

In movement
33, 34 Albertina, Vienna
35 © Iwan Baan
36 Gion A. Caminada

Temporal rhythms
37   Arno Brandlhuber
38   Erica Overmeer
39   Gaudenz Danuser
40-43   Franziska Wittmann

Feeling safe
44-47   Franziska Wittmann
48   © Archive Olgiati
49   Ben Koechlin, Roman Keller

References

Abel, Alexandra / Rudolf, Bernd: Architektur wahrnehmen, Bielefeld 2018.

Alberti, Leon Battista: Ten books on architecture, Joseph Rykwert (ed.), London 1955.

Alexander, Christopher et al.: A Pattern Language, New York 1977.

Anzieu, Didier: Das Haut-Ich, Frankfurt a.M. 1991.

Arnheim, Rudolf: The Dynamics of architectural form, Berkeley 1977.

Bachelard, Gaston: The poetics of space, Boston 1994.

Benjamin, Walter: Über Städte und Architekturen, Detlev Schöttker (ed.), Berlin 2017.

Blaser, Werner: Peter Zumthor Klangkörper Schweiz Expo 2000 Hannover, Konzept für den Schweizer Pavillon, Füllinsdorf 1999.

Blesser, Barry / Salter, Linda-Ruth: spaces speak, are you listening?, Cambridge/London 2007.

Bollnow, Otto Friedrich: Human Space, London 2011.

Brandes, Ralf / Lang, Florian / Schmidt, Robert F. (eds.): Physiologie des Menschen, Berlin 2019.

Bürgin, Matthias / Maag, Trond: Klang vor Ort, in: Stadtklang, Zurich 2016.

Conrads, Ulrich / Leitner, Bernhard: Audible Space, in: Daidalos 17, 1985.

Corbin, Alain: The foul and the fragrant, Cambridge 1986.

Crawford, Matthew B.: The World Beyond Your Head, New York 2015.

Crunelle, Marc: Geruchssinn und Architektur, in: Kunst- und Ausstellungshalle der Bundesrepublik Deutschland GmbH (ed.): Das Riechen. Von Nasen, Düften und Gestank, Göttingen 1995.

Day, Christopher: Places of the soul. Wellingborough 1990.

Eberle, Dietmar / Aicher, Florian: The Temperature of Architecture, Basel 2016.

Eickhoff, Hajo: Himmelsthron und Schaukelstuhl. Die Geschichte des Sitzens, Munich 1993.

Eliade, Mircea: The sacred and the profane, New York 1961.

Énard, Mathias: Erzähl ihnen von Schlachten, Königen und Elefanten, Berlin 2011.

Franck, Georg / Franck, Dorothea: Architektonische Qualität, Munich 2008.

Frank, Irmgard (ed.): Raum_atmosphärische Informationen, Zurich 2015.

Frank, Irmgard: Space and Smell, in: Spatial Expeditions, GAM architecture magazine 13, 2017.

Freudenthaler, Laura: Die Königin schweigt, Vienna 2017.

Gantenbein, Köbi / Rodewald, Raimund: Arkadien, Landschaften poetisch gestalten, Zurich 2016.

Gerber, Andri / Joanelly, Tibor / Franck, Oya Atalay: Proportionen und Wahrnehmung in Architektur und Städtebau, Berlin 2017.

Gibson, James J.: The senses considered as perceptual systems, Westport 1983.

Girot, Christophe (ed.): Mensch und Baum, Zurich 2013.

Grandjean, Etienne: Wohnphysiologie. Grundlagen gesunden Wohnens, Zurich 1973.

Hall, Edward T.: The hidden dimension. Man's use of space in public and private. London 1966.

Hauskeller, Michael (ed.): Die Kunst der Wahrnehmung. Beiträge zu einer Philosophie der sinnlichen Erkenntnis, Zug 2003.

Holmsted Olesen, Christian: Wegner – just one good chair, Ostfildern 2014.

Hönig, Roderick (ed.): Klangkörperbuch, Basel 2000.

Jäkel, Angelika: Gestik des Raumes. Zur leiblichen Kommunikation zwischen Benutzer und Raum in der Architektur, Berlin 2013.

Jütte, Robert: A history oft the senses, Cambridge 2005.

Kruse, Lenelis: Räumliche Umwelt, Berlin 1974.

Kükelhaus, Hugo: Fassen, fühlen, bilden, Organerfahrungen im Umgang mit Phänomenen, Cologne 1975.

Le Corbusier: Toward an architecture, Los Angeles 2007.

Mack, Gerhard: Herzog & de Meuron. The Complete Works, Basel 2013.

McLuhan, Marshall / Powers, Bruce R.: Visual and Acoustic space, in: McLuhan, Marshall / Powers, Bruce R.: The Global Village, Oxford 1989.

Maurer, Bruno / Oechslin, Werner (eds.): Ernst Gisel Architekt, Zurich 2010.

Meisenheimer, Wolfgang: Das Denken des Leibes und der architektonische Raum, Cologne 2004.

Merleau-Ponty, Maurice: Phenomenology of perception, Routledge 2013.

Metzger, Christoph: Architektur und Resonanz, Berlin 2015.

Meyer, Jürgen: Kirchenakustik, Frankfurt a.M. 2003.

Neuenschwander, Eduard: Architektur als Umwelt, Zurich 2013.

Neutra, Richard und Dion: Bauen und die Sinneswelt, 2., erweiterte Auflage, Berlin/Hamburg 1980.

Neutra, Richard: Life and human habitat, Stuttgart 1957.

Olgiati, Valerio, (mit Himmelreich, Jorg und Wiegelmann, Andrea): Auf der Suche nach nichtreferenzieller Architektur, in: archithese 4, 2015.

Olgiati Valerio / Breitschmid, Markus: Non-Referential Architecture, Basel 2018.

Palladio, Andrea: The four books on architecture, New York 1965.

Pallasmaa, Juhani: The eyes of the skin, Chichester 2012.

Pauly, Danièle: Barragan, Space and shadow, walls and colour, Basel 2002.

Pöppel, Ernst: Der Rahmen. Ein Blick des Gehirns auf unser Ich, Munich/Vienna 2006.

Rahm, Philippe / Décosterd, Jean-Gilles: Décosterd & Rahm. Physiological architecture, Basel 2002.

Rasmussen, Steen Eiler: Experiencing Architecture, London 1959.

Rosa, Hartmut: Resonanz. Eine Soziologie der Weltbeziehung, Berlin 2016.

Rossi, Aldo: A scientific autobiography, Cambridge 1981.

Rybczynski, Witold: Wohnen. Über den Verlust der Behaglichkeit, Munich 1987.

Schlorhofer, Bettina (ed.): Cul zuffel e l'aura dado, Gion A. Caminada, Lucerne 2005.

Schmarsow, August: Das Wesen der architektonischen Schöpfung, in: Moravánszky, Akos: Architekturtheorie im 20. Jahrhundert, Vienna 2003, p. 153 ff.

Schmitz, Hermann: Der Leib, der Raum und die Gefühle, Bielefeld 2015.

Schönhammer, Rainer: Einführung in die Wahrnehmungspsychologie. Sinne, Körper, Bewegung, Vienna 2009.

Selle, Gert: Die eigenen vier Wände. Zur verborgenen Geschichte des Wohnens, Frankfurt a.M. 1993.

Sennett, Richard: Flesh and Stone, New York 1994.

Sonderegger, Christina: Der Stadttraum vom Berghaus. Chasa Crestas in Vignogn im Lugnez von Gion A. Caminada, in: tec21 44, 2002.

Straus, Erwin: Vom Sinn der Sinne, Berlin 1956.

Sturm, Ulrike / Bürgin, Matthias: Stadtklang, Zurich 2016.

Tanizaki Jun'ichiro: In praise of shadows, Rutland 1984.

Taut, Bruno: Das japanische Haus und sein Leben, Manfred Speidel (ed.), Berlin 1997.

Vitruv: Ten books on architecture, Cambridge 1999.

Wagner, Anselm / Eckhard, Petra et al.: Spatial Expeditions, GAM Magazine 13, 2017.

Waldenfels, Bernhard: Sinnesschwellen, Frankfurt a.M. 1999.

Wansch, Franz: Wohnen mit Körper, Geist und Seele, Reinbek 1989.

Wittmann, Franziska: Leistungen der Architektur, Lucerne 2017.

Wittmann, Franziska: Resonanz der Architektur, in: werk 7/8, 2018.

Zumthor, Peter: Thinking architecture, Basel 2006.

Zumthor, Peter: Atmospheres, Basel 2006.

Zumthor, Peter: Peter Zumthor 1985-2013, ed. by Thomas Durisch, Zurich 2014.

Biographies

Gion A. Caminada is an architect and Professor of Architecture and Design at the ETH Zurich.

Franziska Wittmann, born in 1985, is an architect and Assistant at the Chair of Gion A. Caminada. She studied Architecture in Munich and Zurich following her training in Dance and Choreography in Salzburg. Her work is based on the assumption that a conscious approach to physical laws of nature and physiological aspects creates qualities with respect to living in spaces. «Being human» in spaces, living, is initially grasped as accommodating oneself in the encounter between physics and physiology.

Acknowledgements

Special thanks to Silvan Blumenthal, Gion A. Caminada, Stefanie and Ariel Koechlin, Lorenz Jaisli, Gisela Monot and Sebastian Schemm.

Thanks to the Department of Architecture of the ETH Zurich for its financial support.